FRIEDRICH DÜRRENMATT

THE PHYSICISTS

Translated from the German by
JAMES KIRKUP

JONATHAN CAPE
THIRTY BEDFORD SQUARE LONDON

Translated from the German *Die Physiker*
© 1962 by Peter Schifferli, Verlags AG 'Die Arche', Zurich
This translation first published in Great Britain 1964
Reissued in this format 1973
This translation © 1963 by James Kirkup

Jonathan Cape Ltd, 30 Bedford Square, London WC1

ISBN Hardback 0 224 00916 8
Paperback 0 224 00913 3

PRINTED IN GREAT BRITAIN
BY LOWE AND BRYDONE (PRINTERS) LTD
THETFORD, NORFOLK

CAPE PLAYS

THE PHYSICISTS

by the same author

plays

THE VISIT

PLAY STRINDBERG

THE METEOR

fiction

THE JUDGE AND HIS HANGMAN

THE PLEDGE

A DANGEROUS GAME

ONCE A GREEK . . .

CHARACTERS

FRÄULEIN DOKTOR MATHILDE VON ZAHND	Alienist
MARTA BOLL	Head Nurse
MONIKA STETTLER	Nurse
UWE SIEVERS	Chief Male Attendant
MCARTHUR	Male Attendant
MURILLO	Male Attendant
HERBERT GEORG BEUTLER ('NEWTON')	Patient
ERNST HEINRICH ERNESTI ('EINSTEIN')	Patient
JOHANN WILHELM MÖBIUS	Patient
OSKAR ROSE	A Missionary
FRAU LINA ROSE	His Wife
ADOLF-FRIEDRICH WILFRIED-KASPAR JÖRG-LUKAS	Their Sons
RICHARD VOSS	Inspector of Police
POLICE DOCTORS	
GUHL	Policeman
BLOCHER	Policeman

ACT ONE

The drawing-room of a comfortable though somewhat dilapidated 'villa' belonging to the private sanatorium known as 'Les Cerisiers'. Surroundings: in the immediate neighbourhood, an unspoilt lakeside which gradually deteriorates into a built-up area and then into a medium-sized or even smaller town. This formerly neat and charming little spot with its castle and Old Town is now adorned by the hideous edifices of insurance companies and exists chiefly on account of a modest university with a recently added theological faculty and summer courses in foreign languages; in addition there are a business college and a Dental School, a boarding-school for young ladies and light industries of no great importance: the town for the most part steers clear of the hurly-burly of modern life.

So the landscape is, in a superficial way, restful to the nerves; there are blue mountain-ranges, hills geometrically afforested and a fairly large lake, as well as a broad plain, once a dismal moor, which turns misty in the evening and is now criss-crossed by canals and irrigation-ditches and is therefore very fertile. There is a house of correction somewhere in the vicinity which has undertaken large-scale agricultural schemes, so that everywhere there are to be seen silent and shadowy bands and little groups of criminals hoeing and digging. Yet these general surroundings really play no part in what follows, and are only mentioned in order to lend precision to the setting, the 'villa' of the madhouse (alas, the word slipped out).

Even there, we never leave the drawing-room, and we have decided to adhere strictly to the Aristotelian unities of place, time and action. The action takes place among madmen and therefore requires a classical framework to keep it in shape.

The 'villa' was where once all the patients of the establishment's

7

founder, Fräulein Doktor Mathilde von Zahnd, were housed – decayed aristocrats, arterio-sclerotic politicians (unless still in office), debilitated millionaires, schizophrenic writers, manic-depressive industrial barons and so on: in short, the mentally disturbed elite of half the western world, for the Fräulein Doktor is a very celebrated person, not just because the hunchbacked spinster in her eternal white coat is descended from a great and very ancient family, of which she is the last presentable member, but because she is also a philanthropist and a psychiatrist of enormous repute; one might almost call her world-famous – her correspondence with C. G. Jung has just been published.

But now the distinguished but not always very pleasant patients have been transferred long since to the elegant, light and airy new building, where for terrific fees even the most disastrous past experiences are turned into blissful memories. The new building spreads over the southern section of the extensive park, branching out into various wings and pavilions (stained-glass windows by Erni in the chapel) that descend towards the plain, while the 'villa's' lawns, dotted with gigantic trees, slope down to the lake. There is a stone embankment along the edge of the lake.

Now only three patients at the very most occupy the drawing-room of the sparsely inhabited 'villa': as it happens, they are all three physicists, though this is not entirely due to chance, for humane principles are put into practice here, and it is felt that 'birds of a feather' should 'flock together'. They live for themselves, each one wrapped in the cocoon of his own little world of the imagination; they take their meals together in the drawing-room, from time to time discuss scientific matters or just sit gazing dully before them – harmless, lovable lunatics, amenable, easily handled and unassuming. In fact, they would be model patients were it not that certain serious, nay, hideous events have recently taken place: three months ago, one of them throttled a nurse, and now the very same thing has just happened again. So once more the police are back in the house and the drawing-room is more than usually animated.

The dead nurse is lying on the parquet floor in a tragic and quite unmistakable attitude, somewhat in the background, so as not to distress the public too much. But it is impossible not to see that a struggle has taken place. The furniture is in great disorder. A standard lamp and two chairs have been knocked over, and left downstage a round table has been over-turned so that it presents only its legs to the spectator.

Apart from all this, the transformation into an asylum has left painful traces on the salon. (The villa was once the Zahnd summer residence.) The walls have been covered to a height of six feet with hygienic, wash-able, glossy paint: above this, the original plaster emerges, with some remnants of stucco mouldings. The three doors in the background, which lead from a small hall into the physicists' sick-rooms, are upholstered with black leather. Moreover, they are numbered from one to three. To the left of the little hall is an ugly central-heating unit; to the right there is a washbasin with towels on a rail.

The sound of a violin, with piano accompaniment, comes from Room Number 2 (the middle room). Beethoven. Kreutzer Sonata. To the left is the wall overlooking the park, with very high windows that reach right down to the linoleum-covered parquet floor. Heavy curtains hang to right and left of the high windows. The glass doors lead on to a terrace, whose stone balustrade is silhouetted against the green of the park and the relatively sunny November light. It is a little after half past four in the afternoon. To the right, over a fireplace which is never used and is covered by a wire guard, there hangs the portrait of an old man with a pointed beard, enclosed in a heavy, gilded frame. Downstage right, a massive oak door. A ponderous chandelier is suspended from the brown, coffered ceiling.

Furniture: beside the round table there stand – when the room is in order – three chairs, all painted white like the table. The remaining fur-niture, with well-worn upholstery, belongs to various periods. Down-stage right, a sofa and a small table flanked by two easy chairs. The standard lamp should really be behind the sofa, when the room should not appear overcrowded. Little is required for the furnishing of a stage on which, contrary to the plays of the ancients, the satire precedes the tragedy. We can begin.

Police officials in plain clothes are busied round the corpse: stolid, good-natured fellows who have already downed a glass or two of white wine: their breaths smell of it. In the centre of the drawing-room stands the INSPECTOR OF POLICE, RICHARD VOSS, *wearing coat and hat;*

on the left is the head nurse, MARTA BOLL, looking as resolute as she really is. In the arm-chair on the far right sits a policeman taking everything down in shorthand. The inspector takes a cigar out of a brown leather cigar case.

INSPECTOR. All right if I smoke?

SISTER BOLL. It's not usual.

INSPECTOR. I beg your pardon.

(*He puts the cigar back in the case.*)

SISTER BOLL. A cup of tea?

INSPECTOR. No brandy?

SISTER BOLL. You're in a medical establishment.

INSPECTOR. Then nothing. Blocher, you can take the photographs now.

BLOCHER. Yes, sir.

(*He begins taking photographs. Flashes.*)

INSPECTOR. What was the nurse's name?

SISTER BOLL. Irene Straub.

INSPECTOR. Age?

SISTER BOLL. Twenty-two. From Kohlwang.

INSPECTOR. Relatives?

SISTER BOLL. A brother in Liechentstein.

INSPECTOR. Informed?

SISTER BOLL. By telephone.

INSPECTOR. The murderer?

SISTER BOLL. Please, Inspector – the poor man's ill, you know.

INSPECTOR. Well, the assailant?

SISTER BOLL. Ernst Heinrich Ernesti. We call him Einstein.

INSPECTOR. Why?

SISTER BOLL. Because he thinks he is Einstein.

INSPECTOR (*turns to the police stenographer*). Have you got the statement down, Guhl?

GUHL. Yes, sir.

INSPECTOR. Strangled, doctor?

POLICE DOCTOR. Quite definitely. With the flex of the standard lamp. These madmen often have gigantic reserves of strength. It's phenomenal.

INSPECTOR. Oh. Is that so? In that case I consider it most irresponsible to leave these madmen in the care of female nurses. This is the second murder –

SISTER BOLL. Please, Inspector.

INSPECTOR. – the second accident within three months in the medical establishment known as Les Cerisiers.

(*He takes out a notebook.*)

On the twelfth of August a certain Herbert Georg Beutler, who believes himself to be the great physicist Sir Isaac Newton, strangled Dorothea Moser, a nurse.

(*He puts the notebook back.*)

And in this very room. If they'd had male attendants such a thing would never have happened.

SISTER BOLL. Do you really think so?

INSPECTOR. I do.

SISTER BOLL. Nurse Moser was a member of the League of Lady Wrestlers and Nurse Straub was District Champion of the National Judo Association.

INSPECTOR. And what about you?

SISTER BOLL. Weight-lifter.

INSPECTOR. Now I'd like to see the murderer.

SISTER BOLL. Please, Inspector.

INSPECTOR. I mean – the assailant.

SISTER BOLL. He's playing his fiddle.

INSPECTOR. Doing what?

SISTER BOLL. Can't you hear him?

INSPECTOR. Then kindly request him to stop.

(SISTER BOLL *does not react.*)

I have to ask him some questions.

SISTER BOLL. Definitely not.

INSPECTOR. And why not?

SISTER BOLL. We cannot allow it, on medical grounds. Herr Ernesti has to play his fiddle, and play it now.

INSPECTOR. But damn it, the man's just strangled a nurse!

SISTER BOLL. Inspector. He's not just any man, but a sick man who needs calming down. And because he thinks he is Einstein he can only calm down when he's playing the fiddle.

INSPECTOR. Can I be going mad?

SISTER BOLL. No.

INSPECTOR. I'm getting confused.

(*He wipes the sweat from his forehead.*)

Warm in here.

SISTER BOLL. I don't think so.

INSPECTOR. Sister Boll. Kindly fetch the doctor in charge.

SISTER BOLL. Quite out of the question. The Fräulein Doktor is accompanying Einstein on the piano. Einstein can only calm down when the Fräulein Doktor plays his accompaniments.

INSPECTOR. And three months ago the Fräulein Doktor had to play chess with Sir Isaac Newton, to calm *him* down. We can't have any more of this, Sister. I simply must speak to the doctor in charge.

SISTER BOLL. Certainly –

INSPECTOR. Thank you.

SISTER BOLL. – but you'll have to wait.

INSPECTOR. How long's this fiddling going to last?

SISTER BOLL. Fifteen minutes, an hour. It all depends.

(*The* INSPECTOR *controls his impatience.*)

INSPECTOR. Very well, I'll wait.

(*He roars.*)

I'll wait!

BLOCHER. We're just about finished, sir.

INSPECTOR. So am I.

(*Silence. The* INSPECTOR *wipes his forehead.*)

You can take away the body.

BLOCHER. Very well, sir.

SISTER BOLL. I'll show them the way through the park to the chapel.

(*She opens the french windows. The body is carried out. Equipment also. The* INSPECTOR *takes off his hat and sinks exhaustedly into the easy chair to the left of the sofa. The fiddling continues, with piano accompaniment. Then out of Room Number 3 comes* HERBERT GEORG BEUTLER *in early eighteenth-century costume. He wears a full-bottomed wig.*)

NEWTON. Sir Isaac Newton.

INSPECTOR. Inspector Richard Voss.

(*He remains seated.*)

NEWTON. I'm so glad. Really very glad. Truly. I heard a noise in here, groans and gurglings, and then people coming and going. May I inquire just what has been going on?

INSPECTOR. Nurse Straub was strangled.

NEWTON. The District Champion of the National Judo Association?

INSPECTOR. The District Champion.

NEWTON. Gruesome.

INSPECTOR. By Ernst Heinrich Ernesti.

NEWTON. But he's playing his fiddle.

INSPECTOR. He has to calm himself down.

NEWTON. The tussle must have taken it out of him. He's rather highly-strung, poor boy. How did he – ?

INSPECTOR. With the cord of the standard lamp.

NEWTON. With the cord of the standard lamp. Yes. That's another possibility. Poor Ernesti. I'm sorry for him. Truly sorry. And I'm sorry for the Ladies' Judo Champion too. Now you'll have to excuse me. I must put things straight.

INSPECTOR. Do. We've got everything we want.

(NEWTON *rights the table and chairs.*)

NEWTON. I simply can't stand disorder. Really it was my love of order that made me become a physicist – (*he rights the standard lamp*) – to interpret the apparent disorder of Nature in the light of a more sublime order. (*He lights a cigarette.*) Will it disturb you if I smoke?

INSPECTOR. On the contrary, I was just thinking ...

(*He takes a cigar out of his case.*)

NEWTON. Excuse me, but we were talking about order just now,

13

so I must tell you that the patients are allowed to smoke here but not the visitors. If they did it would stink the place out.

INSPECTOR. I see.

(*He puts the cigar away.*)

NEWTON. Will it disturb you if I have a nip of brandy?

INSPECTOR. No. Not at all.

(*From behind the wire guard in front of the fire* NEWTON *takes a bottle of brandy and a glass.*)

NEWTON. That poor Ernesti. I'm really upset. How on earth could anyone bring himself to strangle a nurse?

(*He sits down on the sofa and pours out a glass of brandy.*)

INSPECTOR. I believe you strangled one yourself.

NEWTON. Did I?

INSPECTOR. Nurse Dorothea Moser.

NEWTON. The lady wrestler?

INSPECTOR. On the twelfth of August. With the curtain cord.

NEWTON. But that was something quite different, Inspector. I'm not mad, you know. Your health.

INSPECTOR. And yours.

(NEWTON *drinks.*)

NEWTON. Dorothea Moser. Let me cast my mind back. Blonde hair. Enormously powerful. Yet, despite her bulk, very flexible. She loved me and I loved her. It was a dilemma that could only be resolved by the use of a curtain cord.

INSPECTOR. Dilemma?

NEWTON. My mission is to devote myself to the problems of gravitation, not the physical requirements of a woman.

INSPECTOR. Quite.

NEWTON. And then there was this tremendous difference in our ages.

INSPECTOR. Granted. You must be well on the wrong side of two hundred.

(NEWTON *stares at him uncomprehendingly.*)

NEWTON. How do you mean?

INSPECTOR. Well, being Sir Isaac Newton –

NEWTON. Are you out of your mind, Inspector, or are you just having me on?

INSPECTOR. Now look –

NEWTON. Do you really think I'm Sir Isaac Newton?

INSPECTOR. Well, don't you?

(NEWTON *looks at him suspiciously*.)

NEWTON. Inspector, may I tell you a secret? In confidence?

INSPECTOR. Of course.

NEWTON. Well, it's this. I am not Sir Isaac Newton. I only pretend to be Sir Isaac Newton.

INSPECTOR. What for?

NEWTON. So as not to confuse poor Ernesti.

INSPECTOR. I don't get it.

NEWTON. You see, unlike me, Ernesti is really sick. He thinks he's Albert Einstein.

INSPECTOR. But what's that got to do with you?

NEWTON. Well, if Ernesti were to find out that *I* am the real Albert Einstein, all hell would be let loose.

INSPECTOR. Do you mean to say –

NEWTON. I do. I am he. The celebrated physicist and discoverer of the theory of relativity, born March 14th, 1879, in the city of Ulm.

(*The* INSPECTOR *rises in some confusion of mind*.)

INSPECTOR. How do you do?

(NEWTON *also rises*.)

NEWTON. Just call me – Albert.

INSPECTOR. And you can call me Richard.

(*They shake hands*.)

NEWTON. I could give you a Kreutzer with a good deal more dash than Ernesti. The way he plays the Andante – simply barbarous! Simply barbarous!

INSPECTOR. I don't understand anything about music.

NEWTON. Let's sit down, shall we?

(*He draws the* INSPECTOR *down beside him on the sofa*. NEWTON *puts his arm around the* INSPECTOR's *shoulders*.)

NEWTON. Richard.

INSPECTOR. Yes, Albert?

NEWTON. You're cross, aren't you, because you can't arrest me?

INSPECTOR: But Albert –

NEWTON. Is it because I strangled the nurse that you want to arrest me, or because it was I who paved the way for the atomic bomb?

INSPECTOR. But Albert –

NEWTON. When you work that switch by the door, what happens, Richard?

INSPECTOR. The light goes on.

NEWTON. You establish an electrical contact. Do you understand anything about electricity, Richard?

INSPECTOR. I am no physicist.

NEWTON. I don't understand much about it either. All I do is to elaborate a theory about it on the basis of natural observation. I write down this theory in the mathematical idiom and obtain several formulae. Then the engineers come along. They don't care about anything except the formulae. They treat electricity as a pimp treats a whore. They simply exploit it. They build machines – and a machine can only be used when it becomes independent of the knowledge that led to its invention. So any fool nowadays can switch on a light or touch off the atomic bomb.

(*He pats the* INSPECTOR'*s shoulders.*)

And that's what you want to arrest me for, Richard. It's not fair.

INSPECTOR. But I don't want to arrest you, Albert.

NEWTON. It's all because you think I'm mad. But, if you don't understand anything about electricity, why don't you refuse to turn on the light? It's you who are the criminal, Richard. But I must put my brandy away; if Sister Boll comes there will be wigs on the green.

(NEWTON *hides the bottle of brandy behind the wire guard in front of the fire, but leaves the glass where it is.*)

Well, goodbye.

INSPECTOR. Goodbye, Albert.

NEWTON. Oh, Richard. You're the one who should be arrested.
(*He disappears into Room Number 3.*)

INSPECTOR. Now I *will* have a smoke.
(*He takes a cigar firmly out of his cigar case, lights it and smokes. BLOCHER comes through the french windows.*)

BLOCHER. We're ready to leave, sir.
(*The INSPECTOR stamps his foot.*)
Yes, sir.
(*The INSPECTOR calms down and growls.*)

INSPECTOR. Go back to town with the men, Blocher. I'll come on later. I'm waiting for the doctor in charge !

BLOCHER. Very well, sir.
(BLOCHER *goes.*
The INSPECTOR *puffs out great clouds of smoke, stands up, goes to the chimney-piece and stands looking at the portrait. Meanwhile the violin and piano have stopped. The door to Room Number 2 opens and* FRÄULEIN DOKTOR MATHILDE VON ZAHND *comes out. She is hunchbacked, about fifty-five, wearing a white surgical overall-coat and stethoscope.*)

FRL. DOKTOR. My father, August von Zahnd, Privy Councillor. He used to live in this villa before I turned it into a sanatorium. He was a great man, a real person. I am his only child. He hated me like poison; indeed he hated everybody like poison. And with good reason, for as an expert in economics, he saw, revealed in human beings, abysses which are for ever hidden from psychiatrists like myself. We alienists are still hopelessly romantic philanthropists.

INSPECTOR. Three months ago there was a different portrait hanging here.

FRL. DOKTOR. That was my uncle, the politician. Chancellor Joachim von Zahnd.
(*She lays the music score on the small table in front of the sofa.*)
Well, Ernesti has calmed down. In the end he just flung himself on the bed and fell sound asleep. Like a little boy, not a

17

care in the world. I can breathe again: I was afraid he'd want to fiddle through the entire Brahms G Major Sonata.

(*She sits in the arm-chair left of sofa.*)

INSPECTOR. Excuse me, Fräulein Doktor, for smoking in here. I gather it's prohibited, but –

FRL. DOKTOR. Smoke away as much as you like, Inspector. I badly need a cigarette myself; Sister or no Sister. Give me a light.

(*He lights her cigarette and she smokes.*)

Poor Nurse Straub. Simply frightful. She was such a neat, pretty little thing.

(*She notices the glass.*)

Newton?

INSPECTOR. I had the pleasure of speaking to him.

FRL. DOKTOR. I'd better put it away.

INSPECTOR. Allow me.

(*The* INSPECTOR *forestalls her and puts the glass away.*)

FRL. DOKTOR. On account of Sister Boll, you know.

INSPECTOR. I know.

FRL. DOKTOR. So you had a talk with Sir Isaac?

INSPECTOR. Yes, and I discovered something.

(*He sits on the sofa.*)

FRL. DOKTOR. Congratulations.

INSPECTOR. Newton thinks he is really Einstein.

FRL. DOKTOR. That's what he tells everybody. But in fact he really believes he is Newton.

INSPECTOR (*taken aback*). Are you sure?

FRL. DOKTOR. It is I who decide who my patients think they are. I know them far better than they know themselves.

INSPECTOR. Maybe so. In that case you should co-operate with us, Fräulein Doktor. The authorities are complaining.

FRL. DOKTOR. The public prosecutor?

INSPECTOR. Fuming.

FRL. DOKTOR. As if it were my business, Inspector.

INSPECTOR. But two murders –

18

FRL. DOKTOR. Please, Inspector.

INSPECTOR. Two accidents in three months. You must admit that the safety precautions in your establishment would seem inadequate.

FRL. DOKTOR. What sort of safety precautions have you in mind, Inspector? I am the director of a medical establishment, not a reformatory. One can't very well lock murderers up *before* they have committed their murders, can one?

INSPECTOR. It's not a question of murderers but of madmen, and they can commit murders at any time.

FRL. DOKTOR. So can the sane; and, significantly, a lot more often. I have only to think of my grandfather, Leonidas von Zahnd, the Field-Marshal who lost every battle he ever fought. What age do you think we're living in? Has medical science made great advances or not? Do we have new resources at our disposal, drugs that can transform raving madmen into the gentlest of lambs? Must we start putting the mentally sick into solitary confinement again, hung up in nets, I shouldn't wonder, with boxing gloves on, as they used to? As if we were still unable to distinguish between dangerous patients and harmless ones.

INSPECTOR. You weren't much good at distinguishing between them in the cases of Beutler and Ernesti.

FRL. DOKTOR. Unfortunately, no. *That's* what disturbs me, not the fuming of your public prosecutor.

(EINSTEIN *comes out of Room Number 2, carrying his violin. He is lean with long, snow-white hair and moustache.*)

EINSTEIN. I just woke up.

FRL. DOKTOR. Oh, Professor !

EINSTEIN. Did I play well?

FRL. DOKTOR. Beautifully, Professor.

EINSTEIN. What about Nurse Irene? Is she –

FRL. DOKTOR. Don't give it another thought, Professor.

EINSTEIN. I'm going back to bed.

FRL. DOKTOR. Yes, do, Professor.

(EINSTEIN *goes back into his room. The* INSPECTOR *has jumped to his feet.*)

INSPECTOR. So that was him!

FRL. DOKTOR. Yes. Ernst Heinrich Ernesti.

INSPECTOR. The murderer –

FRL. DOKTOR. Please, Inspector.

INSPECTOR. I mean, the assailant, the one who thinks he's Einstein. When was he brought in?

FRL. DOKTOR. Two years ago.

INSPECTOR. And Sir Isaac Newton?

FRL. DOKTOR. One year ago. Both incurable. Look here, Voss, I'm no beginner, God knows, at this sort of job. You know that, and so does the public prosecutor; he has always respected my professional opinion. My sanatorium is world-famous and the fees are correspondingly high. Errors of judgment and incidents that bring the police into my house are luxuries I cannot afford. If anything was to blame here, it was medical science, not me. These incidents could not have been foreseen; you or I would be just as likely to strangle a nurse. No – medically speaking there is no explanation for what has happened. Unless –

(*She has taken a fresh cigarette. The* INSPECTOR *lights it for her.*)
Inspector. Haven't you noticed something?

INSPECTOR. What do you mean?

FRL. DOKTOR. Consider these two patients.

INSPECTOR. Yes?

FRL. DOKTOR. They're both physicists. Nuclear physicists.

INSPECTOR. Well?

FRL. DOKTOR. Inspector, you really have a very unsuspecting mind.
(*The* INSPECTOR *ponders.*)

INSPECTOR. Doktor von Zahnd.

FRL. DOKTOR. Well, Voss?

INSPECTOR. You don't think –

FRL. DOKTOR. They were both doing research on radioactive materials.

INSPECTOR. You suppose there was some connection?

FRL. DOKTOR. I suppose nothing. I merely state the facts. Both of them go mad, the conditions of both deteriorate, both become a danger to the public and both of them strangle their nurses.

INSPECTOR. And you think the radioactivity affected their brains?

FRL. DOKTOR. I regret to say that is a possibility I must face up to.

(*The* INSPECTOR *looks about him.*)

INSPECTOR. What's on the other side of the hall?

FRL. DOKTOR. The green drawing-room and upstairs.

INSPECTOR. How many patients have you got here now?

FRL. DOKTOR. Three.

INSPECTOR. Only three?

FRL. DOKTOR. The rest were transferred to the new wing immediately after the first incident. Fortunately I was able to complete the building just in time. Rich patients contributed to the costs. So did my own relations. They died off one by one, most of them in here. And I was left sole inheritor. Destiny, Voss. I am always sole inheritor. My family is so ancient, it's something of a miracle, in medicine, that I should be relatively normal, I mean, mentally.

(*The* INSPECTOR *thinks a moment.*)

INSPECTOR. What about the third patient?

FRL. DOKTOR. He's also a physicist.

INSPECTOR. Well, that's extraordinary. Don't you think so?

FRL. DOKTOR. Not at all. I put them all together. The writers with the writers, the big industrialists with the big industrialists, the millionairesses with the millionairesses and the physicists with the physicists.

INSPECTOR. What's his name?

FRL. DOKTOR. Johann Wilhelm Möbius.

INSPECTOR. Was he working with radioactive materials as well?

FRL. DOKTOR. No.

INSPECTOR. Mightn't he also perhaps –

FRL. DOKTOR. He's been fifteen years here. He's harmless. His condition has never changed.

INSPECTOR. Doktor von Zahnd, you can't get away with it like that. The public prosecutor insists that your physicists have male attendants.

FRL. DOKTOR. They shall have them.

(*The* INSPECTOR *picks up his hat.*)

INSPECTOR. Good. I'm glad you see it that way. This is the second visit I have paid to Les Cerisiers, Fräulein Doktor. I hope I shan't have to pay a third. Goodbye.

(*He puts on his hat, goes out left through the french windows on to the terrace and makes his way across the park.* DOKTOR MATHILDE VON ZAHND *gazes thoughtfully after him. Enter right the* SISTER, MARTA BOLL, *who stops short, sniffing the air. She is carrying a patient's dossier.*)

SISTER BOLL. Please, Fräulein Doktor.

FRL. DOKTOR. Oh, I'm sorry.

(*She stubs out her cigarette.*)

FRL. DOKTOR. Have they laid out Nurse Straub?

SISTER BOLL. Yes, under the organ-loft.

FRL. DOKTOR. Have candles and wreaths put round her.

SISTER BOLL. I've already telephoned the florists about it.

FRL. DOKTOR. How is my Great-Aunt Senta?

SISTER BOLL. Restless.

FRL. DOKTOR. Double her dose. And my Cousin Ulrich?

SISTER BOLL. No change.

FRL. DOKTOR. Fräulein Sister Boll, I regret to say that one of our traditions here at Les Cerisiers must come to an end. Until now I have employed female nurses only. From tomorrow the villa will be in the hands of male attendants.

SISTER BOLL. Fräulein Doktor von Zahnd. I won't let my three physicists be snatched away from me. They are my most interesting cases.

FRL. DOKTOR. My decision is final.

SISTER BOLL. I'd like to know where you are going to find three male nurses, what with the demand for them these days.

FRL. DOKTOR. That's my problem. Leave it to me. Has Frau
Möbius arrived?

SISTER BOLL. She's waiting in the green drawing-room.

FRL. DOKTOR. Send her in.

SISTER BOLL. Here is Möbius's dossier.

(SISTER BOLL *gives her the dossier and then goes to the door on
the right, where she turns.*)

But –

FRL. DOKTOR. Thank you, Sister, thank you.

(SISTER BOLL *goes. The* DOKTOR *opens the dossier and studies it
at the round table,* SISTER BOLL *comes in again right leading*
FRAU ROSE *and three boys of fourteen, fifteen and sixteen. The
eldest is carrying a brief-case.* HERR ROSE, *a missionary, brings
up the rear. The* DOKTOR *stands up.*)

My dear Frau Möbius –

FRAU ROSE. Rose. Frau Rose. It must be an awful surprise to you,
Fräulein Doktor, but three weeks ago I married Herr Rose,
who is a missionary. It was perhaps rather sudden. We met in
September at a missionary convention.

(*She blushes and rather awkwardly indicates her new husband.*)

Oskar was a widower.

(*The* FRÄULEIN DOKTOR *shakes her by the hand.*)

FRL. DOKTOR. Congratulations, Frau Rose, heartiest congratulations. And my best wishes to you, too, Herr Rose.

(*She gives him a friendly nod.*)

FRAU ROSE. You do understand why we took this step?

FRL. DOKTOR. But of course, Frau Rose. Life must continue to
bloom and flourish.

HERR ROSE. How peaceful it is here! What a friendly atmosphere!
Truly a divine peace reigns over this house, just as the psalmist
says: For the Lord heareth the needy and despiseth not his
prisoners.

FRAU ROSE. Oskar is such a good preacher, Fräulein Doktor.

(*She blushes.*)

My boys.

FRL. DOKTOR. Good afternoon, boys.

THREE BOYS. Good afternoon, Fräulein Doktor.

(*The youngest picks something up from the floor.*)

JÖRG-LUKAS. A piece of electric wire, Fräulein Doktor. It was lying on the floor.

FRL. DOKTOR. Thank you, young man. Grand boys you have, Frau Rose. You can face the future with confidence.

(FRAU ROSE *sits on the sofa to the right, the* DOKTOR *at the table left. Behind the sofa the three boys, and on the chair at extreme right,* HERR ROSE.)

FRAU ROSE. Fräulein Doktor, I have brought my boys with me for a very good reason. Oskar is taking over a mission in the Marianas.

HERR ROSE. In the Pacific Ocean.

FRAU ROSE. I thought it only proper that my boys should make their father's acquaintance before their departure. This will be their one and only opportunity. They were still quite small when he fell ill and now, perhaps, they will be saying good-bye for ever.

FRL. DOKTOR. Frau Rose, speaking as a doctor, I would say that there might be objections, but speaking as a human being I can understand your wish and gladly give my consent to a family reunion.

FRAU ROSE. And how is my dear little Johann Wilhelm?

(*The* DOKTOR *leafs through the dossier.*)

FRL. DOKTOR. Our dear old Möbius shows signs neither of improvement nor of relapse, Frau Rose. He's spinning his own little cocoon.

FRAU ROSE. Does he still claim to see King Solomon?

FRL. DOKTOR. Yes.

HERR ROSE. A sad and deplorable delusion.

FRL. DOKTOR. Your harsh judgment surprises me a bit, Herr Missionary. Nevertheless, as a theologian you must surely reckon with the possibility of a miracle.

HERR ROSE. Oh, of course – but not in the case of someone mentally sick.

24

FRL. DOKTOR. Whether the manifestations perceived by the mentally sick are real or not is something which psychiatry is not competent to judge. Psychiatry has to concern itself exclusively with states of mind and with the nerves, and in this respect things are in a bad enough way with our dear old Möbius, even though his illness takes rather a mild form. As for helping him, goodness me, another course of insulin shock treatment might be indicated, but as the others have been without success I'm leaving it alone. I can't work miracles, Frau Rose, and I can't pamper our dear old Möbius back to health; but I certainly don't want to make his life a misery either.

FRAU ROSE. Does he know that I've – I mean, does he know about the divorce?

FRL. DOKTOR. He has been told the facts.

FRAU ROSE. Did he understand?

FRL. DOKTOR. He takes hardly any interest in the outside world any more.

FRAU ROSE. Fräulein Doktor. Try to understand my position. I am five years older than Johann Wilhelm. I first met him when he was a fifteen-year-old schoolboy, in my father's house, where he had rented an attic room. He was an orphan and wretchedly poor. I helped him through high school and later made it possible for him to read physics at the university. We got married on his twentieth birthday, against my parents' wishes. We worked day and night. He was writing his dissertation and I took a job with a transport company. Four years later we had our eldest boy, Adolf-Friedrich, and then came the two others. Finally there were prospects of his obtaining a professorship; we thought we could begin to relax at last. But then Johann Wilhelm fell ill and his illness swallowed up immense sums of money. To provide for my family I went to work in a chocolate factory. Tobler's chocolate factory.

(*She silently wipes away a tear.*)

For years I worked my fingers to the bone.

(*They are all moved.*)

FRL. DOKTOR. Frau Rose, you are a brave woman.

HERR ROSE. And a good mother.

FRAU ROSE. Fräulein Doktor, until now I have made it possible for Johann Wilhelm to stay in your establishment. The fees are far beyond my means, but God came to my help time and time again. All the same, I am now, financially speaking, at the end of my tether. I simply cannot raise the extra money.

FRL. DOKTOR. That's understandable, Frau Rose.

FRAU ROSE. I'm afraid now you'll think I married Oskar so as to get out of providing for Johann Wilhelm. But that is not so. Things will be even more difficult for me now. Oskar brings me six sons from his previous marriage!

FRL. DOKTOR. Six?

HERR ROSE. Six.

FRAU ROSE. Six. Oskar is a most zealous father. But now there are nine boys to feed and Oskar is by no means robust. And his salary is not high.

(She weeps.)

FRL. DOKTOR. Come, now, Frau Rose, you mustn't. Don't cry.

FRAU ROSE. I reproach myself bitterly for having left my poor little Johann Wilhelm in the lurch.

FRL. DOKTOR. Frau Rose! You have no need to reproach yourself.

FRAU ROSE. My poor little Johann Wilhelm will have to go into a state institution now.

FRL. DOKTOR. No he won't, Frau Rose. Our dear old Möbius will stay on here in the villa. You have my word. He's got used to being here and has found some nice, kind colleagues. I'm not a monster, you know!

FRAU ROSE. You're so good to me, Fräulein Doktor.

FRL. DOKTOR. Not at all, Frau Rose, not at all. There are such things as grants and bequests. There's the Oppel Foundation for invalid scientists, there's the Doktor Steinemann Bequest. Money's as thick as muck around here and it's my duty as his doctor to pitchfork some of it in the direction of your dear little Johann Wilhelm. You can steam off to the Marianas with a clear conscience. But now let us have a word with Möbius himself – our dear, good old Möbius.

(*She goes and opens the door Number* 1. FRAU ROSE *rises expectantly.*)

Dear Möbius. You have visitors. Now leave your physicist's lair for a moment and come in here.

(JOHANN WILHELM MÖBIUS *comes out of Room Number* 1. *He is about forty, a rather clumsy man. He looks around him uncertainly, stares at* FRAU ROSE, *then at the boys and finally at the missionary,* HERR ROSE. *He appears not to recognize them and remains silent.*)

FRAU ROSE. Johann Wilhelm!

THREE BOYS. Papa!

(MÖBIUS *remains silent.*)

FRL. DOKTOR. My dear Möbius, you're not going to tell me you don't recognize your own wife?

(MÖBIUS *stares at* FRAU ROSE.)

MÖBIUS. Lina?

FRL. DOKTOR. That's better, Möbius. Of course it's Lina.

MÖBIUS. Hullo, Lina.

FRAU ROSE. My little Johann Wilhelm, my dear, dear little Johann Wilhelm.

FRL. DOKTOR. There we are, now. Frau Rose, Herr Rose, if you have anything else to tell me I shall be at your disposal in the new wing over there.

(*She goes off through door left.*)

FRAU ROSE. These are your sons, Johann Wilhelm.

(MÖBIUS *starts.*)

MÖBIUS. Three?

FRAU ROSE. Of course, Johann Wilhelm. Three.

(*She introduces the boys to him.*)

Adolf-Friedrich, your eldest.

(MÖBIUS *shakes his hand.*)

MÖBIUS. How do you do, Adolf-Friedrich, my eldest.

ADOLF-FRIEDRICH. How do you do, Papi.

MÖBIUS. How old are you, Adolf-Friedrich?

ADOLF-FRIEDRICH. Sixteen, Papi.

MÖBIUS. What do you want to be?

ADOLF-FRIEDRICH. A minister, Papi.

MÖBIUS. I remember now. We were walking across St Joseph's Square. I was holding your hand. The sun was shining brightly and the shadows were just as if they'd been drawn with a compass.

(MÖBIUS *turns to the next boy.*)

And you – you are – ?

WILFRIED-KASPAR. My name is Wilfried-Kaspar, Papi.

MÖBIUS. Fourteen?

WILFRIED-KASPAR. Fifteen. I should like to study philosophy.

MÖBIUS. Philosophy?

FRAU ROSE. He's an exceptionally mature boy for his age.

WILFRIED-KASPAR. I have read Schopenhauer and Nietzsche.

FRAU ROSE. This is your youngest boy, Jörg-Lukas. Fourteen.

JÖRG-LUKAS. How do you do, Papi.

MÖBIUS. How do you do, Jörg-Lukas, my youngest.

FRAU ROSE. He's the one who takes after you most.

JÖRG-LUKAS. I want to be a physicist, Papi.

(MÖBIUS *stares at his youngest in horror.*)

MÖBIUS. A physicist?

JÖRG-LUKAS. Yes, Papi.

MÖBIUS. You mustn't, Jörg-Lukas. Not under any circumstances. You get that idea right out of your head. I – I forbid it!

(JÖRG-LUKAS *looks puzzled.*)

JÖRG-LUKAS. But you became a physicist yourself, Papi –

MÖBIUS. I should never have been one, Jörg-Lukas. Never. I wouldn't be in the madhouse now.

FRAU ROSE. But Johann Wilhelm. That's not right. You are in a sanatorium, not a madhouse. You're having a little trouble with your nerves, that's all.

(MÖBIUS *shakes his head.*)

28

MÖBIUS. No, Lina. People say I am mad. Everybody. Even you. And my boys too. Because King Solomon appears to me.
(*They are all struck dumb with embarrassment. Then* FRAU ROSE *introduces* HERR ROSE.)

FRAU ROSE. Let me introduce Oskar Rose to you, Johann Wilhelm. He is my husband. A missionary.

MÖBIUS. Your husband? But *I'm* your husband.

FRAU ROSE. Not any more, my little Johann Wilhelm.
(*She blushes.*)
We're divorced, you know.

MÖBIUS. Divorced?

FRAU ROSE. Now you know that, surely?

MÖBIUS. No.

FRAU ROSE. Doktor von Zahnd told you. Of course she did.

MÖBIUS. Possibly.

FRAU ROSE. And then I married Oskar. He has six boys of his own. He was a minister at Guttannen and now he has been given a post in the Marianas.

MÖBIUS. In the Marianas?

HERR ROSE. In the Pacific Ocean.

FRAU ROSE. We're joining the ship at Bremen tomorrow.

MÖBIUS. I see.
(*He stares at* HERR ROSE. *They are all embarrassed.*)

FRAU ROSE. Yes, that's right.
(MÖBIUS *nods to* HERR ROSE.)

MÖBIUS. I am glad to make the acquaintance of my boys' new father.

HERR ROSE. I have taken them to my bosom, Herr Möbius, all three of them. God will provide. As the psalmist says: The Lord is my shepherd, I shall not want.

FRAU ROSE. Oskar knows all the psalms off by heart. The Psalms of David, the Psalms of Solomon.

MÖBIUS. I am glad the boys have found such an excellent father. I have not been a satisfactory father to them.
(*The three boys protest at this.*)

THREE BOYS. Ah, no, Papi.

MÖBIUS. And Lina has found a husband more worthy of her.

FRAU ROSE. But my dear little Johann Wilhelm –

MÖBIUS. I congratulate you. Heartiest congratulations.

FRAU ROSE. We must be going soon.

MÖBIUS. To the Marianas.

FRAU ROSE. I mean, we must say goodbye to one another.

MÖBIUS. For ever.

FRAU ROSE. Your sons are remarkably musical, Johann Wilhelm. They are very gifted players on their recorders. Play your papi something, boys, as a parting present.

THREE BOYS. Yes, mama.

(ADOLF-FRIEDRICH *opens the brief-case and distributes recorders.*)

FRAU ROSE. Sit down, my little Johann Wilhelm.

(MÖBIUS *sits down at the round table.* FRAU ROSE *and* HERR ROSE *sit down on the sofa. The boys take their places in the middle of the room.*)

Now. What are you going to play?

JÖRG-LUKAS. A bit of Buxtehude.

FRAU ROSE. Ready – one, two, three.

(*The boys play.*)

More feeling, boys, more expression!

(*The boys play with more expression.* MÖBIUS *jumps up.*)

MÖBIUS. I'd rather they didn't. Please, don't!

(*The boys stop playing, bewildered.*)

Don't play any more. Please. For King Solomon's sake. Don't play any more.

FRAU ROSE. But Johann Wilhelm!

MÖBIUS. Please, don't play any more. Please, don't play any more, please, please.

HERR ROSE. Herr Möbius. King Solomon himself will rejoice to hear the piping of these innocent lads. Just think: Solomon, the Psalmist, Solomon, the singer of the Song of Songs.

MÖBIUS. Herr Missionary. I have met Solomon face to face. He is no longer the great golden king who sang of the Shulamite,

and of the two young roes that are twins, which feed among
the roses. He has cast away his purple robe !

(MÖBIUS *suddenly dashes past his horrified family to his room
and throws open the door.*)

Now here in my room he crouches naked and stinking, the
pauper king of truth, and his psalms are horrible. Listen care-
fully, Herr Missionary. You love the words of the psalms and
know them all by heart. Well, you can learn these by heart as
well.

(*He has run to the round table left, turned it over, climbed into it
and sat down.*)

A Song of Solomon to be sung to the Cosmonauts.

> We shagged off into outer space
> To the deserts of the moon. Foundered in her dust
> Right from the start there were plenty
> That soundlessly shot their bolts out there.
> But most of them cooked
> In the lead fumes of Mercury, were wiped out
> In the oil-swamps of Venus and
> Even on Mars we were wolfed by the sun –
> Thundering, radioactive, yellow.
>
> Jupiter stank
> An arrow-swift rotatory methane mash
> He, the almighty, slung over us
> Till we spewed up our guts over Ganymede.

FRAU ROSE. But, Johann Wilhelm –
MÖBIUS.

> Saturn we greeted with curses
> What came next, a waste of breath
>
> Uranus Neptune
> Greyish-green, frozen to death
> Over Pluto and Transpluto fell the final
> Dirty jokes.

We had long since mistaken the sun for Sirius
Sirius for Canopus
Outcasts we cast out, up into the deep
Towards a few white stars
That we never reached anyhow

Long since mummied in our spacecraft
Caked with filth

In our deathsheads no more memories
Of breathing earth.

SISTER BOLL. But Herr Möbius!
> (SISTER BOLL *has entered, right, with* NURSE MONIKA.
> MÖBIUS *sits staring blankly, his face like a mask, inside the
> overturned table.*)

MÖBIUS. And now get yourselves off to the Marianas!

FRAU ROSE. My little Johann Wilhelm –

THREE BOYS. Papi!

MÖBIUS. Get yourselves away! And quick about it! Off to the
Marianas the whole pack of you!
> (*He stands up with a threatening look. The* ROSE *family is non-
> plussed.*)

SISTER BOLL. Come, Frau Rose. Come, boys. Herr Rose. He
needs time to calm down.

MÖBIUS. Away with you! Get out!

SISTER BOLL. Just a mild attack. Nurse Monika will stay with
him and calm him down. Just a mild attack.

MÖBIUS. Get out, will you! For good and all! Off to the Pacific
with the lot of you!

JÖRG-LUKAS. Goodbye, Papi! Goodbye!
> (SISTER BOLL *leads the overwrought and weeping family off
> right.* MÖBIUS *goes on yelling unrestrainedly after them.*)

MÖBIUS. I never want to set eyes on you again! You have insul-
ted King Solomon! May you be damned for ever! May you
and the entire Marianas sink and drown in the Mariana Deep!

Four thousand fathoms down! May you sink and rot in the blackest hole of the sea, forgotten by God and man!

MONIKA. We're alone now. Your family can't hear you any more.

(MÖBIUS *stares wonderingly at* NURSE MONIKA *and finally seems to come to himself.*)

MÖBIUS. Ah, yes, of course.

(NURSE MONIKA *is silent. He is somewhat embarrassed.*)

Was I a bit violent?

MONIKA. Somewhat.

MÖBIUS. I had to speak the truth.

MONIKA. Obviously.

MÖBIUS. I got worked up.

MONIKA. You were putting it on.

MÖBIUS. So you saw through me?

MONIKA. I've been looking after you for two years now.

(*He paces up and down, then stops.*)

MÖBIUS. All right. I admit I was just pretending to be mad.

MONIKA. Why?

MÖBIUS. So that I could say goodbye to my wife and sons for ever.

MONIKA. But why in such a dreadful way?

MÖBIUS. Oh no, it was a humane way. If you're in a madhouse already, the only way to get rid of the past is to behave like a madman. Now they can forget me with a clear conscience. My performance finally cured them of ever wanting to see me again. The consequences for myself are unimportant; life outside this establishment is the only thing that counts. Madness costs money. For fifteen years my Lina has been paying out monstrous sums, and an end had to be put to all that. This was a favourable moment. King Solomon has revealed to me what was to be revealed; the Principle of Universal Discovery is complete, the final pages have been dictated and my wife has found a new husband, a missionary, a good man through and through. You should feel reassured now, nurse. Everything is in order.

(*He is about to go.*)

MONIKA. You had it all planned.

MÖBIUS. I am a physicist.

(*He turns to go to his room.*)

MONIKA. Herr Möbius.

(*He stops.*)

MÖBIUS. Yes, nurse?

MONIKA. I have something to tell you.

MÖBIUS. Well?

MONIKA. It concerns us both.

MÖBIUS. Let's sit down.

(*They sit down: she on the sofa, he in the arm-chair on its left.*)

MONIKA. We must say goodbye to one another too. And for ever.

(*He is frightened.*)

MÖBIUS. Are you leaving me?

MONIKA. Orders.

MÖBIUS. What has happened?

MONIKA. I'm being transferred to the main building. From tomorrow the patients here will be supervised by male attendants. Nurses won't be allowed to enter the villa any more.

MÖBIUS. Because of Newton and Einstein?

MONIKA. At the request of the public prosecutor. Doktor von Zahnd feared there would be difficulties and gave way.

(*Silence. He is dejected.*)

MÖBIUS. Nurse Monika, I don't know what to say. I've forgotten how to express my feelings; talking shop with the two sick men I live with can hardly be called conversation. I am afraid that I may have dried up inside as well. Yet you ought to know that for me everything has been different since I got to know you. It's been more bearable. These were two years during which I was happier than before. Because through you, Nurse Monika, I have found the courage to accept being shut away, to accept the fate of being a madman. Goodbye.

(*He stands, holding out his hand.*)

MONIKA. Herr Möbius, I don't think you *are* mad.

(MÖBIUS *laughs and sits down again.*)

MÖBIUS. Neither do I. But that does not alter my position in any
way. It's my misfortune that King Solomon keeps appearing
to me and in the realm of science there is nothing more repug-
nant than a miracle.

MONIKA. Herr Möbius, I believe in this miracle.

(MÖBIUS *stares at her, disconcerted.*)

MÖBIUS. You believe in it?

MONIKA. I believe in King Solomon.

MÖBIUS. And that he appears to me?

MONIKA. That he appears to you.

MÖBIUS. Day in, day out?

MONIKA. Day in, day out.

MÖBIUS. And you believe that he dictates the secrets of nature to
me? How all things connect? The Principle of Universal Discovery?

MONIKA. I believe all that. And if you were to tell me that
King David and all his court appeared before you I should
believe it all. I simply know that you are not sick. I can
feel it.

(*Silence. Then* MÖBIUS *leaps to his feet.*)

MÖBIUS. Nurse Monika! Get out of here!

(*She remains seated.*)

MONIKA. I'm staying.

MÖBIUS. I never want to see you again.

MONIKA. You need me. Apart from me, you have no one left in
all the world. Not one single person.

MÖBIUS. It is fatal to believe in King Solomon.

MONIKA. I love you.

(MÖBIUS *stares perplexed at* MONIKA, *and sits down again.*
Silence.)

MÖBIUS. I love you too. (*She stares at him.*) That is why you are
in danger. Because we love one another.

(EINSTEIN, *smoking his pipe, comes out of Room Number 2.*)

EINSTEIN. I woke up again. I suddenly remembered.

MONIKA. Now, Herr Professor.

EINSTEIN. I strangled Nurse Irene.

MONIKA. Try not to think about it, Herr Professor.

(*He looks at his hands.*)

EINSTEIN. Shall I ever again be able to touch my violin with these hands?

(MÖBIUS *stands up as if to protect* MONIKA.)

MÖBIUS. You were playing just now.

EINSTEIN. Well, I hope?

MÖBIUS. The Kreutzer Sonata. While the police were here.

EINSTEIN. The Kreutzer! Well, thank God for that!

(*His face, having brightened, clouds over again.*)

All the same, I don't like playing the fiddle and I don't like this pipe either. It's foul.

MÖBIUS. Then give them up.

EINSTEIN. I can't do that, not if I'm Albert Einstein.

(*He gives them both a sharp look.*)

Are you two in love?

MONIKA. We are in love.

(EINSTEIN *proceeds thoughtfully backstage to where the murdered nurse lay.*)

EINSTEIN. Nurse Irene and I were in love too. She would have done anything for me. I warned her. I shouted at her. I treated her like a dog. I implored her to run away before it was too late. In vain. She stayed. She wanted to take me away into the country. To Kohlwang. She wanted to marry me. She even obtained permission for the wedding from Fräulein Doktor von Zahnd herself. Then I strangled her. Poor Nurse Irene. In all the world there's nothing more absurd than a woman's frantic desire for self-sacrifice.

(MONIKA *goes to him.*)

MONIKA. Go and lie down again, Herr Professor.

EINSTEIN. You may call me Albert.

MONIKA. Be sensible, now, Albert.

EINSTEIN. And you be sensible, too, Nurse. Obey the man you
love and run away from him; or you're lost.

(*He turns back towards Room Number 2.*)

I'm going back to bed.

(*He disappears into Room Number 2.*)

MONIKA. That poor, confused creature.

MÖBIUS. Well, he must have convinced you finally of the impos-
sibility of remaining in love with me.

MONIKA. But you're not mad.

MÖBIUS. It would be wiser if you were to treat me as if I were.
Make your escape now! Go on, run! Clear off! Or I'll treat
you like a dog myself.

MONIKA. Why can't you treat me like a woman?

MÖBIUS. Come here, Monika.

(*He leads her to an arm-chair, sits down opposite her and takes
her hands.*)

Listen. I have committed a grave mistake. I have not kept
King Solomon's appearances to myself. So he is making me
atone for it. For life. But you ought not to be punished for
what I did. In the eyes of the world, you are in love with a
man who is mentally sick. You're simply asking for trouble.
Leave this place; forget me: that would be the best thing for
us both.

MONIKA. Don't you want me?

MÖBIUS. Why do you talk like that?

MONIKA. I want to sleep with you, I want to have children by you.
I know I'm talking quite shamelessly. But why won't you
look at me? Don't you find me attractive? I know these
nurses' uniforms are hideous.

(*She tears off her nurse's cap.*)

I hate my profession! For five years I've been looking after
sick people out of love for my fellow-beings. I never flinched;
everyone could count on me: I sacrificed myself. But now I
want to sacrifice myself for one person alone, to exist for one
person alone, and not for everybody all the time. I want to

exist for the man I love. For you. I will do anything you ask, work for you day and night: only you can't send me away! I have no one else in the world! I am as much alone as you.

MÖBIUS. Monika. I must send you away.

MONIKA (*despairing*). But don't you feel any love for me at all?

MÖBIUS. I love you, Monika. Good God, I love you. That's what's mad.

MONIKA. Then why do you betray me? and not only me. You say that King Solomon appears to you. Why do you betray him too?

(MÖBIUS, *terribly worked-up, takes hold of her.*)

MÖBIUS. Monika! You can believe what you like of me. I'm a weakling; all right. I *am* unworthy of your love. But I have always remained faithful to King Solomon. He thrust himself into my life, suddenly, unbidden, he abused me, he destroyed my life, but I have never betrayed him.

MONIKA. Are you sure?

MÖBIUS. Do you doubt it?

MONIKA. You think you have to atone because you have not kept his appearances secret. But perhaps it is because you do not stand up for his revelations.

(*He lets her go.*)

MÖBIUS. I – I don't follow you.

MONIKA. He dictates to you the Principle of Universal Discovery. Why won't you fight for that principle?

MÖBIUS. But after all, people do regard me as a madman.

MONIKA. Why can't you show more spirit?

MÖBIUS. In my case, to show spirit would be a crime.

MONIKA. Johann Wilhelm. I've spoken to Fräulein Doktor von Zahnd.

(MÖBIUS *stares at her.*)

MÖBIUS. You spoke to her?

MONIKA. You are free.

MÖBIUS. Free?

MONIKA. We can get married.

MÖBIUS. God.

MONIKA. Fräulein Doktor von Zahnd has arranged everything. Of course, she still considers you're a sick man, but not dangerous. And it's not a hereditary sickness. She said she was madder than you, and she laughed.

MÖBIUS. That was good of her.

MONIKA. She's a great woman.

MÖBIUS. Indeed.

MONIKA. Johann Wilhelm! I've accepted a post as district nurse in Blumenstein. I've been saving up. We have no need to worry. All we need is to keep our love for each other.

(MÖBIUS *has stood up. It gradually gets darker in the room.*)

Isn't it wonderful?

MÖBIUS. Indeed, yes.

MONIKA. You don't sound very happy.

MÖBIUS. It's all happened so unexpectedly –

MONIKA. I've done something else.

MÖBIUS. What would that be?

MONIKA. I spoke to Professor Schubert.

MÖBIUS. He was my teacher.

MONIKA. He remembered you perfectly. He said you'd been his best pupil.

MÖBIUS. And what did you talk to him about?

MONIKA. He promised he would examine your manuscripts with an open mind.

MÖBIUS. Did you explain that they have been dictated by King Solomon?

MONIKA. Naturally.

MÖBIUS. Well?

MONIKA. He just laughed. He said you'd always been a bit of a joker. Johann Wilhelm! We mustn't think just of ourselves. You are a chosen being. King Solomon appeared to you, revealed himself in all his glory and confided in you the wisdom of the heavens. Now you have to take the way ordained by that miracle, turning neither to left nor right, even if that way leads through mockery and laughter, through disbelief and doubt. But the way leads out of this asylum, Johann Wilhelm, it leads into the outside world, not into loneliness, it leads into battle. I am here to help you, to fight at your side. Heaven, that sent you King Solomon, sent me too.

(MÖBIUS *stares out of the window*.)

Dearest.

MÖBIUS. Yes, dear?

MONIKA. Aren't you happy?

MÖBIUS. Very.

MONIKA. Now we must get your bags packed. The train for Blumenstein leaves at eight twenty.

MÖBIUS. There's not much to pack.

MONIKA. It's got quite dark.

MÖBIUS. The nights are drawing in quickly now.

MONIKA. I'll switch on the light.

MÖBIUS. Wait a moment. Come here.

(*She goes to him. Only their silhouettes are visible*.)

MONIKA. You have tears in your eyes.

MÖBIUS. So have you.

MONIKA. Tears of happiness.

(*He rips down the curtain and flings it over her. A brief struggle. Their silhouettes are no longer visible. Then silence. The door to Room Number 3 opens. A shaft of light shines into the darkened room. In the doorway stands* NEWTON *in eighteenth-century costume.* MÖBIUS *rises*.)

NEWTON. What's happened?

MÖBIUS. I've strangled Nurse Monika Stettler.

(*The sound of a fiddle playing comes from Room Number 2*.)

NEWTON. Einstein's off again. Kreisler. Humoresque.

(*He goes to the fireplace and gets the brandy*.)

ACT TWO

One hour later. The same room. It is dark outside. The police are again present, measuring, sketching, photographing. But this time the corpse of Monika Stettler *cannot be seen by the audience and it is assumed to be lying backstage right, below the window. The drawing-room is brightly lit. The chandelier and the standard lamp have been switched on. On the sofa sits* Fräulein Doktor Mathilde von Zahnd, *looking gloomy and preoccupied. There is a box of cigars on the small table in front of her.* Guhl, *with his stenographer's notebook, is occupying the arm-chair on the extreme right.* Inspector Voss, *wearing his coat and hat, turns away from where the corpse is presumed to be lying and comes downstage.*

FRL. DOKTOR. Cigar?
INSPECTOR. No, thanks.
FRL. DOKTOR. Brandy?
INSPECTOR. Later.
    (*A silence.*)
INSPECTOR. Blocher, you can take your photographs now.
BLOCHER. Very well, Inspector.
    (*Photographs and flashes.*)
INSPECTOR. What was the nurse's name?
FRL. DOKTOR. Monika Stettler.
INSPECTOR. Age?
FRL. DOKTOR. Twenty-five. From Blumenstein.
INSPECTOR. Any relatives?
FRL. DOKTOR. None.
INSPECTOR. Have you got the statement down, Guhl?
GUHL. Yes, sir.

INSPECTOR. Strangled again, doctor?

POLICE DOCTOR. Quite definitely. And again, tremendous strength was used. But with the curtain cord this time.

INSPECTOR. Just like three months ago.

(*He sits down wearily in the arm-chair downstage right.*)

FRL. DOKTOR. Would you like to have the murderer brought in?

INSPECTOR. Please, Fräulein Doktor.

FRL. DOKTOR. I mean, the assailant.

INSPECTOR. I don't think so.

FRL. DOKTOR. But –

INSPECTOR. Fräulein Doktor von Zahnd. I am doing my duty, taking down evidence, examining the corpse, having it photographed and getting the police doctor's opinion. But I do not wish to examine Möbius. I leave him to you. Along with the other radioactive physicists.

FRL. DOKTOR. And the public prosecutor?

INSPECTOR. He's past being angry now. He's just brooding.

(*The* DOKTOR *wipes her forehead.*)

FRL. DOKTOR. Warm in here.

INSPECTOR. *I* don't think so.

FRL. DOKTOR. This third murder –

INSPECTOR. Please, Fräulein Doktor.

FRL. DOKTOR. This third accident is the end as far as my work at Les Cerisiers goes. Now I can resign. Monika Stettler was my best nurse. She understood the patients. She could enter into their states of mind. I loved her like a daughter. But her death is not the worst thing that's happened. My reputation as a doctor is ruined.

INSPECTOR. You'll build it up again. Blocher, get another shot from above.

BLOCHER. Very well, Herr Inspektor.

(*Two enormous male attendants enter right pushing a trolley with food, plates and cutlery on it. One of them is a negro. They are accompanied by a chief male attendant who is equally enormous.*)

42

CHIEF ATTNDT. Dinner for the dear good patients, Fräulein Doktor.
(*The* INSPECTOR *jumps up.*)

INSPECTOR. Uwe Sievers.

CHIEF ATTNDT. Correct, Herr Inspektor. Uwe Sievers. Former
European heavyweight boxing champion. Now chief male
attendant at Les Cerisiers.

INSPECTOR. And these two other bruisers?

CHIEF ATTNDT. Murillo, South American champion, also a
heavyweight. And McArthur (*pointing to the negro*), North
American middleweight champion. McArthur, the table.

(MCARTHUR *rights the overturned table.*)

Murillo, the tablecloth.

(MURILLO *spreads a white cloth over the table.*)

McArthur, the Meissen.

(MCARTHUR *lays the plates.*)

Murillo, the silver.

(MURILLO *lays out the silver.*)

McArthur, the soup-tureen in the middle.

(MCARTHUR *sets the soup-tureen in the centre of the table.*)

INSPECTOR. And what are the dear good patients having for
dinner?

(*He lifts the lid of the tureen.*)

Liver-dumpling soup.

CHIEF ATTNDT. Poulet à la broche. Cordon Bleu.

INSPECTOR. Fantastic.

CHIEF ATTNDT. First class.

INSPECTOR. I am a mere fourteenth-class official. Plain cooking is
all we can run to in my home.

CHIEF ATTNDT. Fräulein Doktor. Dinner is served.

FRL. DOKTOR. Thank you, Sievers. You may go. The patients
will help themselves.

CHIEF ATTNDT. Herr Inspektor. Glad to have made your
acquaintance.

(*The three attendants bow and go out right. The* INSPECTOR *gazes
after them.*)

43

INSPECTOR. Well I'm damned.

FRL. DOKTOR. Satisfied?

INSPECTOR. Envious. If we had them with the police –

FRL. DOKTOR. Their wages are astronomical.

INSPECTOR. With all your industrial barons and multi-million-airesses you can certainly afford such luxuries. Those fellows will finally set the public prosecutor's mind at rest. They wouldn't let anyone slip through their fingers.

(*From Room Number 2 comes the sound of Einstein playing his fiddle.*)

There's Einstein at it again.

FRL. DOKTOR. Kreisler. As usual. Liebesleid. The pangs of love.

BLOCHER. We're finished now, Herr Inspektor.

INSPECTOR. Take the body out. Again.

(*Two policemen lift the corpse. Then* MÖBIUS *rushes out of Room Number 1.*)

MÖBIUS. Monika! My beloved!

(*The two policemen stand still, carrying the corpse.* FRÄULEIN DOKTOR *rises majestically.*)

FRL. DOKTOR. Möbius! How could you do it! You have killed my best nurse, my sweetest nurse!

MÖBIUS. I'm sorry, Fräulein Doktor.

FRL. DOKTOR. Sorry.

MÖBIUS. King Solomon ordained it.

FRL. DOKTOR. King Solomon.

(*She sits down again, heavily. Her face is white.*)

So it was His Majesty who arranged the murder.

MÖBIUS. I was standing at the window staring out into the falling dusk. Then the King came floating up out of the park over the terrace, right up close to me, and whispered his commands to me through the window-pane.

FRL. DOKTOR. Excuse me, Inspector, my nerves.

INSPECTOR. Don't mention it.

FRL. DOKTOR. A place like this wears one out.

INSPECTOR. I can well believe it.

FRL. DOKTOR. If you'll excuse me –
(*She stands up.*)
Herr Inspektor Voss, please express my profound regret to the
public prosecutor for the incidents that have taken place in my
sanatorium. Kindly assure him that everything is now well in
hand again. Doctor, gentlemen, it was a pleasure.
(*She first of all goes upstage right, bows her head ceremoniously
before the corpse, looks at* MÖBIUS *and goes off right.*)
INSPECTOR. There. Now you can take the body into the chapel.
Put her beside Nurse Irene.
MÖBIUS. Monika!
(*The two policemen carrying the corpse and the others carrying
their apparatus go out through the doors to the garden. The police
doctor follows them.*)
Monika, my love.
(*The* INSPECTOR *walks to the small table beside the sofa.*)
INSPECTOR. Möbius, come and sit down. Now I absolutely must
have a cigar. I've earned it.
(*He takes a gigantic cigar out of the box and considers its size.*)
Good grief!
(*He bites off the end and lights the cigar.*)
My dear Möbius, behind the fire-guard you will find a bottle
of brandy hidden away by Sir Isaac Newton.
MÖBIUS. Certainly, Herr Inspektor.
(*The* INSPECTOR *blows out clouds of smoke while* MÖBIUS *goes
and gets the brandy and the glass.*)
May I pour you one?
INSPECTOR. Indeed you may.
(*He takes the glass and drinks.*)
MÖBIUS. Another?
INSPECTOR. Another.
(MÖBIUS *pours out another glass.*)
MÖBIUS. Herr Inspektor, I must ask you to arrest me.
INSPECTOR. But what for, my dear Möbius?
MÖBIUS. Well, after all, Nurse Monika –

45

INSPECTOR. You yourself admitted that you acted under the orders of King Solomon. As long as I'm unable to arrest *him* you are a free man.

MÖBIUS. All the same –

INSPECTOR. There's no question of all the same. Pour me another glass.

MÖBIUS. Certainly, Herr Inspektor.

INSPECTOR. And now hide the brandy bottle away again or the attendants will be getting drunk on it.

MÖBIUS. Very well, Herr Inspektor.

(*He puts the brandy away.*)

INSPECTOR. You see, it's like this. Every year in this small town and the surrounding district, I arrest a few murderers. Not many. A bare half-dozen. Some of these it gives me great pleasure to apprehend; others I feel sorry for. All the same I have to arrest them. Justice is Justice. And then you come along and your two colleagues. At first I felt angry at not being able to proceed with the arrests. But now? All at once I'm enjoying myself. I could shout with joy. I have discovered three murderers whom I can, with an easy conscience, leave unmolested. For the first time justice is on holiday – and it's a terrific feeling. Justice, my friend, is a terrible strain; you wear yourself out in its service, both physically and morally; I need a breathing space, that's all. Thanks to you, my dear Möbius, I've got it. Well, goodbye. Give my kindest regards to Einstein and Newton.

MÖBIUS. Very well, Herr Inspektor.

INSPECTOR. And my respects to King Solomon.

(*The* INSPECTOR *goes.* MÖBIUS *is left alone. He sits down on the sofa and takes his head in his hands.* NEWTON *comes out of Room Number 3.*)

NEWTON. What's cooking?

(MÖBIUS *does not reply.* NEWTON *takes the lid off the tureen.*) Liver-dumpling soup.

(*Lifts the lid off the other dishes on the trolley.*)

46

Poulet à la broche. Cordon Bleu. Extraordinary. We usually only have a light supper in the evenings. And a very modest one. Ever since the other patients were moved into the new building.

(*He helps himself to soup.*)

Lost your appetite?

(MÖBIUS *remains silent.*)

I quite understand. I lost mine too after my nurse.

(*He sits and begins to drink the soup.* MÖBIUS *rises and is about to go to his room.*)

Stay here.

MÖBIUS. Sir Isaac?

NEWTON. I have something to say to you, Möbius.

(MÖBIUS *remains standing.*)

MÖBIUS. Well?

(NEWTON *gestures at the food.*)

NEWTON. Wouldn't you like to try just a spoonful of the liver-dumpling soup? It's excellent.

MÖBIUS. No.

NEWTON. Möbius, we are no longer lovingly tended by nurses, we are being guarded by male attendants. Great hefty fellows.

MÖBIUS. That's of no consequence.

NEWTON. Perhaps not to you, Möbius. It's obvious you really want to spend the rest of your days in a madhouse. But it is of some consequence to me. The fact is, I want to get out of here.

(*He finishes his plate of soup.*)

Mmm – Now for the poulet à la broche.

(*He helps himself.*)

These new attendants have compelled me to act straight away.

MÖBIUS. That's your affair.

NEWTON. Not altogether. A confession, Möbius. I am not mad.

MÖBIUS. But of course not, Sir Isaac.

NEWTON. I am not Sir Isaac Newton.

MÖBIUS. I know. Albert Einstein.

47

NEWTON. Fiddlesticks. Nor am I Herbert Georg Beutler, as
they think here. My real name, dear boy, is Kilton.

(MÖBIUS *stares at him in horror.*)

MÖBIUS. Alec Jaspar Kilton?

NEWTON. Correct.

MÖBIUS. The author of the theory of Equivalents?

NEWTON. The very same.

(MÖBIUS *moves over to the table.*)

MÖBIUS. So you wangled your way in here?

NEWTON. By pretending to be mad.

MÖBIUS. In order to – spy on me?

NEWTON. In order to get to the root of your madness. My im-
peccable German was acquired in our Intelligence Service. A
frightful grind.

MÖBIUS. And because poor Nurse Dorothea stumbled on the
truth, you –

NEWTON. – Yes. I am most extraordinarily sorry about the whole
thing.

MÖBIUS. I understand.

NEWTON. Orders are orders.

MÖBIUS. Of course.

NEWTON. I couldn't do anything else.

MÖBIUS. Naturally.

NEWTON. My whole mission hung in the balance, the most secret
undertaking of our Secret Service. I had to kill, if I wanted
to avert suspicion. Nurse Dorothea no longer considered
me to be demented; Fräulein Doktor von Zahnd thought
I was only slightly touched; to prove my total insanity I had
to commit a murder. I say, this poulet à la broche is simply
superb.

(*Einstein is fiddling in Room Number 2.*)

MÖBIUS. Einstein's at it again.

NEWTON. That Bach Gavotte.

MÖBIUS. His dinner's getting cold.

NEWTON. Let the old idiot get on with his fiddling.

MÖBIUS. Is that a threat?

NEWTON. I have the most immeasurable respect for you. It would grieve me to have to take violent steps.

MÖBIUS. So your mission is to abduct me?

NEWTON. Yes, if the suspicions of our Intelligence Service prove correct.

MÖBIUS. What would they be?

NEWTON. Our Intelligence Service happens to consider you to be the greatest genius among present-day physicists.

MÖBIUS. I'm a man whose nerves are sick, Kilton, that's all.

NEWTON. Our Intelligence Service has other ideas on the subject.

MÖBIUS. And what is your opinion?

NEWTON. I simply consider you to be the greatest physicist of all time.

MÖBIUS. And how did your Intelligence Service get on my trail?

NEWTON. Through me. Quite by chance I read your dissertation on the foundations of a new concept of physics. At first I thought it was a practical joke. Then the scales seemed to fall from my eyes. I realized I was reading the greatest work of genius in the history of physics. I began to make inquiries about its author but made no progress. Thereupon I informed our Intelligence Service: they got on to you.

EINSTEIN. You were not the only one who read that dissertation, Kilton.

(He has entered unnoticed from Room Number 2 with his fiddle and bow under his arm.)

As a matter of fact, I'm not mad either. May I introduce myself? I too am a physicist. Member of a certain Intelligence Service. A somewhat different one from yours, Kilton. My name is Joseph Eisler.

MÖBIUS. The discoverer of the Eisler-effect?

EINSTEIN. The very same.

NEWTON. 'Disappeared' in 1950.

EINSTEIN. Of my own free will.

(NEWTON is suddenly seen to have a revolver in his hand.)

NEWTON. Eisler, might I trouble you to stand with your face to the wall, please?

EINSTEIN. Why of course.

(*He saunters easily across to the window-seat, lays his fiddle and bow on the mantelpiece, then swiftly turns with a revolver in his hand.*)

My dear Kilton, we both, I suspect, know how to handle these things, so don't you think it would be better if we were to avoid a duel? If possible? I shall gladly lay down my Browning if you will do the same with your Colt.

NEWTON. Agreed.

EINSTEIN. Behind the fire-guard with the brandy. Just in case the attendants come in suddenly.

NEWTON. Good.

(*They both put their revolvers behind the fire-guard.*)

EINSTEIN. You've messed up all my plans, Kilton. I thought you really were mad.

NEWTON. Never mind: I thought you were.

EINSTEIN. Things kept going wrong. That business with Nurse Irene, for example, this afternoon. She was getting suspicious, and so she signed her own death-warrant. I am most extraordinarily sorry about the whole thing.

MÖBIUS. I understand.

EINSTEIN. Orders are orders.

MÖBIUS. Of course.

EINSTEIN. I couldn't do anything else.

MÖBIUS. Naturally.

EINSTEIN. My whole mission hung in the balance; it was the most secret undertaking of our Secret Service. But let's sit down.

NEWTON. Yes, let's sit down.

(*He sits down on the left side of the table,* EINSTEIN *on the right.*)

MÖBIUS. Eisler, I presume that you, too, want to compel me now to –

EINSTEIN. Now Möbius –

50

MÖBIUS. – want to persuade me to visit your country.

EINSTEIN. We also consider you to be the greatest physicist of all time. But just at the moment all I'm interested in is my dinner. It's a real gallows-feast.

(*He ladles soup into his plate.*)

Still no appetite, Möbius?

MÖBIUS. Yes; it's suddenly come back. Now that you've both got to the bottom of things.

(*He sits down between them at the table and helps himself to the soup.*)

NEWTON. Burgundy, Möbius?

MÖBIUS. Go ahead.

(NEWTON *pours out the wine.*)

NEWTON. I'll attack the Cordon Bleu, what?

MÖBIUS. Make yourselves perfectly at home.

NEWTON. Bon appétit.

EINSTEIN. Bon appétit.

MÖBIUS. Bon appétit.

(*They eat. The three male attendants come in right, the chief attendant carrying a notebook.*)

CHIEF ATTNDT. Patient Beutler!

NEWTON. Here.

CHIEF ATTNDT. Patient Ernesti!

EINSTEIN. Here.

CHIEF ATTNDT. Patient Möbius!

MÖBIUS. Here.

CHIEF ATTNDT. Head Nurse Sievers, Nurse Murillo, Nurse Mc-Arthur.

(*He puts the notebook away.*)

On the recommendation of the authorities, certain security measures are to be observed. Murillo. The grille.

(MURILLO *lets down a metal grille over the window. The room now suddenly has the aspect of a prison.*)

McArthur. Lock up.

(MCARTHUR *locks the grille.*)

Have the gentlemen any further requests before retiring for the night? Patient Beutler?

NEWTON. No.

CHIEF ATTNDT. Patient Ernesti?

EINSTEIN. No.

CHIEF ATTNDT. Patient Möbius?

MÖBIUS. No.

CHIEF ATTNDT. Gentlemen, we take our leave. Good night.

(*The three attendants go. Silence.*)

EINSTEIN. Monsters.

NEWTON. They've got more of the brutes lurking in the park. I've been watching them from my window for some time.

(EINSTEIN *goes up and inspects the grille.*)

EINSTEIN. Solid steel. With a special lock.

(NEWTON *goes to the door of his room, opens it and looks in.*)

NEWTON. They've put a grille over my window. Quick work.

(*He opens the other two doors.*)

Same for Eisler. And for Möbius.

(*He goes to the door right.*)

Locked.

(*He sits down again. So does* EINSTEIN.)

EINSTEIN. Prisoners.

NEWTON. Only logical. What with our nurses and everything.

EINSTEIN. We'll never get out of this madhouse now unless we act together.

MÖBIUS. I do not wish to escape.

EINSTEIN. Möbius –

MÖBIUS. I see no reason for it at all. On the contrary. I am quite satisfied with my fate.

(*Silence.*)

NEWTON. But I'm not satisfied with it. That's a fairly decisive element in the case, don't you think? With all respect to your personal feelings, you are a genius and therefore common property. You mapped out new directions in physics. But you haven't a monopoly of knowledge. It is your duty to open the doors for us, the non-geniuses. Come on out: within a year, we'll have you in a top hat, white tie and tails, fly you to Stockholm and give you the Nobel prize.

MÖBIUS. Your Intelligence Service is very altruistic.

NEWTON. I don't mind telling you, Möbius, they have a suspicion that you've solved the problem of gravitation.

MÖBIUS. I have.

(*Silence.*)

EINSTEIN. You say that as if it were nothing.

MÖBIUS. How else should I say it?

EINSTEIN. *Our* Intelligence Service believed you would discover the Unitary Theory of Elementary Particles.

MÖBIUS. Then I can set their minds at rest as well. I have discovered it.

(NEWTON *mops his forehead.*)

NEWTON. The basic formula.

EINSTEIN. It's ludicrous. Here we have hordes of highly-paid physicists in gigantic state-supported laboratories working for years and years and years vainly trying to make some progress in the realm of physics while you do it quite casually at your desk in this madhouse.

(*He too mops his forehead.*)

NEWTON. Möbius. What about the – the Principle of Universal Discovery?

MÖBIUS. Yes, something on those lines, too. I did it out of curiosity, as a practical corollary to my theoretical investigations. Why play the innocent? We have to face the consequences of our scientific thinking. It was my duty to work out the effects that would be produced by my Unitary Theory of Elementary Particles and by my discoveries in the field of gravitation. The result is – devastating. New and inconceivable forces would be unleashed, making possible a technical advance that would transcend the wildest flights of fantasy if my findings were to fall into the hands of mankind.

EINSTEIN. And that can scarcely be avoided.

53

NEWTON. The only question is: who's going to get at them first?
(MÖBIUS *laughs*.)

MÖBIUS. You'd like that for your own Intelligence Service, wouldn't you, Kilton, and the military machine behind it?

NEWTON. And why not? It seems to me, if it can restore the greatest physicist of all time to the confraternity of the physical sciences, any military machine is a sacred instrument. It's nothing more nor less than a question of the freedom of scientific knowledge. It doesn't matter who guarantees that freedom. I give my services to any system, providing that system leaves me alone. I know there's a lot of talk nowadays about physicists' moral responsibilities. We suddenly find ourselves confronted with our own fears and we have a fit of morality. This is nonsense. We have far-reaching, pioneering work to do and that's all that should concern us. Whether or not humanity has the wit to follow the new trails we are blazing is its own look-out, not ours.

EINSTEIN. Admittedly we have pioneer work to do. I believe that too. But all the same we cannot escape our responsibilities. We are providing humanity with colossal sources of power. That gives us the right to impose conditions. If we are physicists, then we must become power politicians. We must decide in whose favour we shall apply our knowledge, and I for one have made my decision. Whereas you, Kilton, are nothing but a lamentable aesthete. If you feel so strongly about the freedom of knowledge why don't you come over to our side? We too for some time now have found it impossible to dictate to our physicists. We too need results. Our political system too must eat out of the scientist's hand.

NEWTON. Both our political systems, Eisler, must now eat out of Möbius's hand.

EINSTEIN. On the contrary. He must do what we tell him. We have finally got him in check.

NEWTON. You think so? It looks more like stalemate to me. Our Intelligence Services, unfortunately, both hit upon the same idea. So don't let's delude ourselves. Let's face the impossible situation we've got ourselves into. If Möbius goes with you, I can't do anything about it because you would stop me. And similarly you would be helpless if Möbius decided in my favour. It isn't we who have the choice, it's him.

(EINSTEIN *rises ceremoniously.*)

EINSTEIN. Let us retrieve our revolvers.

(NEWTON *rises likewise.*)

NEWTON. Let us do battle.

(NEWTON *brings the two revolvers and hands* EINSTEIN *his weapon.*)

EINSTEIN. I'm sorry this affair is moving to a bloody conclusion. But we must fight it out, between us and then with the attendants. If need be with Möbius himself. He may well be the most important man in the world, but his manuscripts are more important still.

MÖBIUS. My manuscripts? I've burnt them.

(*Dead silence.*)

EINSTEIN. Burnt them?

MÖBIUS (*embarrassed*). I had to. Before the police came back. So as not to be found out.

(EINSTEIN *bursts into despairing laughter.*)

EINSTEIN. Burnt.

(NEWTON *screams with rage.*)

NEWTON. Fifteen years' work.

EINSTEIN. I shall go mad.

NEWTON. Officially, you already are.

(*They put their revolvers in their pockets and sit down, utterly crushed, on the sofa.*)

EINSTEIN. We've played right into your hands, Möbius.

NEWTON. And to think that for this I had to strangle a nurse and learn German !

EINSTEIN. And I had to learn to play the fiddle. It was torture for someone like me with no ear for music.

MÖBIUS. Shall we go on with dinner?

NEWTON. I've lost my appetite.

EINSTEIN. Pity about the Cordon Bleu.

(MÖBIUS *stands*.)

MÖBIUS. Here we are, three physicists. The decision we have to make is one that we must make as physicists; we must go about it therefore in a scientific manner. We must not let ourselves be influenced by personal feelings but by logical processes. We must endeavour to find a rational solution. We cannot afford to make mistakes in our thinking, because a false conclusion would lead to catastrophe. The basic facts are clear. All three of us have the same end in view, but our tactics differ. Our aim is the advancement of physics. You, Kilton, want to preserve the freedom of that science, and argue that it has no responsibility but to itself. On the other hand you, Eisler, see physics as responsible to the power politics of one particular country. What is the real position now? That's what I must know if I have to make a decision.

NEWTON. Some of the world's most famous physicists are waiting to welcome you. Remuneration and accommodation could not be better. The climate is murderous, but the air-conditioning is excellent.

MÖBIUS. But are these physicists free men?

NEWTON. My dear Möbius, these physicists declare they are ready to solve scientific problems which are decisive for the defence of the country. Therefore, you must understand –

MÖBIUS. So they are not free.

(*He turns to* EINSTEIN.)

Joseph Eisler, your line is power politics. But that requires power. Have you got it?

EINSTEIN. You misunderstand me, Möbius. My political power, to be precise, lies in the fact that I have renounced my own power in favour of a political party.

MÖBIUS. Would you be able to persuade that party to take on your responsibility, or is there a risk of the party persuading you?

56

EINSTEIN. Möbius, that's ridiculous. I can only hope that the party will follow my recommendations, nothing more. In any case, without hope, all political systems are untenable.

MÖBIUS. Are your physicists free at least?

EINSTEIN. Well, naturally, they too are needed for the defence of the country –

MÖBIUS. Extraordinary. Each of you is trying to palm off a different theory, yet the reality you offer me is the same in both cases: a prison. I'd prefer the madhouse. Here at least I feel safe from the exactions of power politicians.

EINSTEIN. But after all, one must take certain risks.

MÖBIUS. There are certain risks that one may not take: the destruction of humanity is one. We know what the world has done with the weapons it already possesses; we can imagine what it would do with those that my researches make possible, and it is these considerations that have governed my conduct. I was poor. I had a wife and three children. Fame beckoned from the university; industry tempted me with money. Both courses were too dangerous. I should have had to publish the result of my researches, and the consequences would have been the overthrow of all scientific knowledge and the breakdown of the economic structure of our society. A sense of responsibility compelled me to choose another course. I threw up my academic career, said no to industry and abandoned my family to its fate. I took on the fool's cap and bells. I let it be known that King Solomon kept appearing to me, and before long, I was clapped into a madhouse.

NEWTON. But that couldn't solve anything.

MÖBIUS. Reason demanded the taking of this step. In the realm of knowledge we have reached the farthest frontiers of perception. We know a few precisely calculable laws, a few basic connections between incomprehensible phenomena and that is all. The rest is mystery closed to the rational mind. We have reached the end of our journey. But humanity has not yet got as far as that. We have battled onwards, but now no one is following in our footsteps; we have encountered a void. Our knowledge has become a frightening burden. Our researches are perilous, our discoveries are lethal. For us physicists there is nothing left but to surrender to reality. It has not kept up with us. It disintegrates on touching us. We have to take back our knowledge and I have taken it back. There is no other way out, and that goes for you as well.

EINSTEIN. What do you mean by that?

MÖBIUS. You must stay with me here in the madhouse.

NEWTON. What! Us?

MÖBIUS. Both of you.

(*Silence.*)

NEWTON. But Möbius, surely you can't expect us to – for the rest of our days to –

MÖBIUS. I expect you have secret radio transmitters.

EINSTEIN. Well?

MÖBIUS. You inform your superior that you have made a mistake, that I really am mad.

EINSTEIN. Then we'd be stuck here for the rest of our lives. Nobody's going to lose any sleep over a broken-down spy.

MÖBIUS. But it's the one chance I have to remain undetected. Only in the madhouse can we be free. Only in the madhouse can we think our own thoughts. Outside they would be dynamite.

NEWTON. But damn it all, we're not mad.

MÖBIUS. But we *are* murderers.

(*They stare at him in perplexity.*)

NEWTON. I resent that!

EINSTEIN. You shouldn't have said that, Möbius!

MÖBIUS. Anyone who takes life is a murderer, and we have taken life. Each of us came to this establishment for a definite purpose. Each of us killed his nurse, again for a definite purpose. You two did it so as not to endanger the outcome of your secret mission; and I, because Nurse Monika believed in me. She thought I was an unrecognized genius. She did not realize that today it's the duty of a genius to remain unrecognized. Killing is a terrible thing. I killed in order to avoid an even more dreadful murder. Then you come along. I can't do away with you, but perhaps I can bring you round to my way of thinking. Are those murders we committed to stand for nothing? Either they were sacrificial killings, or just plain murders. Either we stay in this madhouse or the world becomes one. Either we wipe ourselves out of the memory of mankind or mankind wipes out itself.

(*Silence.*)

NEWTON. Möbius!

MÖBIUS. Kilton.

NEWTON. This place. These ghastly male attendants. That hunchback of a doctor!

MÖBIUS. Well?

EINSTEIN. We're caged in, like wild beasts!

MÖBIUS. We are wild beasts. We ought not to be let loose on humanity.

(*Silence.*)

NEWTON. Is there really no other way out?

MÖBIUS. None.

(*Silence.*)

EINSTEIN. Johann Wilhelm Möbius, I am a man of integrity. I'm staying.

(*Silence.*)

NEWTON. I'm staying too, for ever.

(*Silence.*)

MÖBIUS. Thank you. Thank you for leaving the world this faint chance of survival.

(*He raises his glass.*)

To our nurses!

(*They have gravely risen to their feet.*)

NEWTON. I drink to Dorothea Moser.

THE OTHERS. Nurse Dorothea!

NEWTON. Dorothea! You had to be sacrificed. In return for your love, I gave you death! Now I want to prove myself worthy of you.

EINSTEIN. I drink to Irene Straub!

THE OTHERS. Nurse Irene!

EINSTEIN. Irene! You had to be sacrificed. As a tribute to your memory and your devotion, I am now going to behave like a rational human being.

MÖBIUS. I drink to Monika Stettler.

THE OTHERS. Nurse Monika!

MÖBIUS. Monika! You had to be sacrificed. May your love bless the friendship which we three have formed in your name. Give us the strength to be fools, that we may guard faithfully the secrets of our knowledge.

(*They drink and put the glasses on the table.*)

NEWTON. Let us be changed to madmen once again. Let us put on the shade of Newton.

EINSTEIN. Let us once again scrape away at Kreisler and Beethoven.

MÖBIUS. Let us have King Solomon appear before us once again.

NEWTON. Let us be mad, but wise.

EINSTEIN. Prisoners but free.

MÖBIUS. Physicists but innocent.

(*The three of them wave to each other and go back to their rooms. The drawing-room stands empty. Then enter right MCARTHUR and MURILLO. They are now wearing black uniforms, peaked caps and pistols. They clear the table. MCARTHUR wheels the trolley with the china and cutlery off right. MURILLO places the round table in front of the window right, and puts on it the upturned chairs, as if the place were a restaurant closing for the night. Then MURILLO goes off right. The room stands empty again. Then enters right FRÄULEIN DOKTOR MATHILDE VON ZAHND. As usual she is wearing a white surgical coat. Stethoscope. She looks about her. Finally SIEVERS comes in, also wearing a black uniform.*)

SIEVERS. Yes, boss?

FRL. DOKTOR. Sievers, the portrait.

(McARTHUR *and* MURILLO *carry in a large oil-painting, a portrait in a heavy gilded frame. It represents a general.* SIEVERS *takes down the old portrait and hangs up the new one.*)

It's better for General Leonidas von Zahnd to be hung in here than among the women patients. He still looks a great man, the old war-horse, despite his goitre. He loved heroic deaths and that is what there have been in this house.

(*She gazes at her father's portrait.*)

And so the Privy Councillor must go into the women's section among the millionairesses. Put him in the corridor for the time being.

(McARTHUR *and* MURILLO *carry out the picture right.*)

Has my general administrator arrived with his minions?

CHIEF ATTNDT. They are waiting in the green drawing-room. Shall I serve champagne and caviare?

FRL. DOKTOR. That gang's here to work, not stuff its guts.

(*She sits down on the sofa.*)

Have Möbius brought in, Sievers.

CHIEF ATTNDT. Sure, boss.

(*He goes to Room Number* I. *Opens door.*)

Möbius, out!

(MÖBIUS *appears. He is exalted.*)

MÖBIUS. A night of prayer. Deep blue and holy. The night of the mighty king. His white shadow is loosed from the wall; his eyes are shining.

(*Silence.*)

FRL. DOKTOR. Möbius, on the orders of the public prosecutor I may speak to you only in the presence of an attendant.

MÖBIUS. I understand, Fräulein Doktor.

FRL. DOKTOR. What I have to say to you applies also to your colleagues.

(McARTHUR *and* MURILLO *have returned.*)

McArthur and Murillo. Fetch the other two.

(McARTHUR *and* MURILLO *open doors Numbers* 2 *and* 3.)

61

MURILLO AND MCARTHUR. Out!

(NEWTON *and* EINSTEIN *come out, also in a state of exaltation.*)

NEWTON. A night of secrets. Unending and sublime. Through the bars of my window glitter Jupiter and Saturn unveiling the laws of the infinite.

EINSTEIN. A blessed night. Comforting and good. Riddles fall silent, questions are dumb. I should like to play on for ever.

FRL. DOKTOR. Alec Jaspar Kilton and Joseph Eisler –

(*They both stare at her in amazement.*)

I have something to say to you.

(*They both draw their revolvers but are disarmed by* MURILLO *and* MCARTHUR.)

Gentlemen, your conversation was overheard; I had had my suspicions for a long time. McArthur and Murillo, bring in their secret radio transmitters.

CHIEF ATTNDT. Hands behind your heads!

(MÖBIUS, EINSTEIN *and* NEWTON *put their hands behind their heads while* MCARTHUR *and* MURILLO *go into rooms Numbers 2 and 3.*)

NEWTON. It's funny!

(*He laughs. The others do not. Spooky.*)

EINSTEIN. I don't know.

NEWTON. Too funny!

(*He laughs again, then falls silent.* MCARTHUR *and* MURILLO *come in with the transmitters.*)

CHIEF ATTNDT. Hands down.

(*The physicists obey. Silence.*)

FRL. DOKTOR. Sievers. The searchlights.

CHIEF ATTNDT. Okay, boss.

(*He raises his hand. Searchlights blaze in from outside, bathing the physicists in a blinding light. At the same time,* SIEVERS *switches off the lights in the room.*)

FRL. DOKTOR. The villa is surrounded by guards. Any attempt to escape would be useless.

(*To the attendants.*)

You three, get out!

(*The three attendants leave the room, carrying the revolvers and radio apparatus. Silence.*)

You alone shall hear my secret. You alone among men. Because it doesn't matter any longer whether you know or not.

(*Silence.*)

(*Grandly*) He has appeared before me also. Solomon, the golden king.

(*All three stare at her in perplexity.*)

MÖBIUS. Solomon?

FRL. DOKTOR. This many a long year.

(NEWTON *softly giggles.*)

(*Unconcerned*) The first time was in my study. One summer evening. Outside, the sun was still shining, and a woodpecker was hammering away somewhere in the park. Then suddenly the golden king came floating towards me like a tremendous angel.

EINSTEIN. She's gone mad.

FRL. DOKTOR. His gaze came to rest upon me. His lips parted. He began to converse with his handmaiden. He had arisen from the dead, he desired to take upon himself again the power that once belonged to him here below, he had unveiled his wisdom, that Möbius might reign on earth, in his name.

EINSTEIN. She must be locked up. She should be in a madhouse.

FRL. DOKTOR. But Möbius betrayed him. He tried to keep secret what could not be kept secret. For what was revealed to him was no secret. Because it could be thought. Everything that can be thought is thought at some time or another. Now or in the future. What Solomon had found could be found by anyone, but he wanted it to belong to himself alone, his means towards the establishment of his holy dominion over all the world. And so he did seek me out, his unworthy handmaiden.

EINSTEIN (*insistently*). You – are – mad. D'you hear, you – are – mad.

FRL. DOKTOR. He did command me to cast down Möbius, and reign in his place. I hearkened unto his command. I was a doctor and Möbius was my patient. I could do with him whatever I wished. Year in, year out, I fogged his brain and made photocopies of the golden king's proclamations, down to the last page.

NEWTON. You're raving mad! Absolutely! Get this clear once and for all! (*Softly*) We're all mad.

FRL. DOKTOR. I went cautiously about my work. At first I exploited only two or three discoveries, in order to rake in the necessary capital. Then I founded enormous plants and factories, one after the other. I've created a giant cartel. I shall exploit to the full, gentlemen, the Principle of Universal Discovery.

MÖBIUS (*insistent*). Fräulein Doktor Mathilde von Zahnd, you are sick. Solomon does not exist. He never appeared to me.

FRL. DOKTOR. Liar.

MÖBIUS. I only pretended to see him in order to keep my discoveries secret.

FRL. DOKTOR. You deny him.

MÖBIUS. Do be reasonable. Don't you see you're mad?

FRL. DOKTOR. I'm no more mad than you.

MÖBIUS. Then I must shout the truth to the whole world. You sucked me dry all these years, without shame. You even let my poor wife go on paying for me.

FRL. DOKTOR. You are powerless, Möbius. Even if your voice were to reach the outside world, nobody would believe you. Because to the public at large you are nothing but a dangerous lunatic. By the murder you committed.

(*The truth dawns on the three men.*)

MÖBIUS. Monika –

EINSTEIN. Irene –

NEWTON. Dorothea –

FRL. DOKTOR. I simply seized my opportunity. The wisdom of Solomon had to be safeguarded and your treachery punished.

I had to render all three of you harmless. By the murders you committed. I drove those three nurses into your arms. I could count upon your reactions. You were as predictable as automata. You murdered like professionals.

(Möbius *is about to throw himself upon her but is restrained by* Einstein.)

There's no point in attacking me, Möbius. Just as there was no point in burning manuscripts which I already possess in duplicate.

(Möbius *turns away*.)

What you see around you are no longer the walls of an asylum. This is the strong room of my trust. It contains three physicists, the only human beings apart from myself to know the truth. Those who keep watch over you are not medical attendants. Sievers is the head of my works police. You have taken refuge in a prison you built for yourselves. Solomon thought through you. He acted through you. And now he destroys you, through me.

(*Silence.*)

But I'm taking his power upon myself. I have no fears. My sanatorium is full of my own lunatic relatives, all of them loaded with jewels and medals. I am the last normal member of my family. No more. The last one. I am barren. I can love no one. Only humanity. And so King Solomon took pity on me. He, with his thousand brides, chose me. Now I shall be mightier than my forefathers. My cartel will dictate in each country, each continent; it will ransack the solar system and thrust out beyond the great nebula in Andromeda. It all adds up, and the answer comes out in favour, not of the world, but of an old hunchbacked spinster.

(*She rings a little bell and the* Chief Attendant *comes in right*.)

CHIEF ATTNDT. Yes, boss?

FRL. DOKTOR. I must go, Sievers. The board of trustees is waiting. Today we go into world-wide operation. The assembly lines are rolling.

(She goes out right with CHIEF ATTENDANT. *The three physicists are alone. Silence. It is all over. Stillness.)*

NEWTON. It is all over.

(He sits down on the sofa.)

EINSTEIN. The world has fallen into the hands of an insane, female psychiatrist.

(He sits down beside NEWTON.)

MÖBIUS. What was once thought can never be unthought.

*(*MÖBIUS *sits down in the arm-chair on the left of the sofa. Silence. The three stare before them. Then each speaks in turn, quite calmly and naturally, simply introducing themselves to the audience.)*

NEWTON. I am Newton. Sir Isaac Newton. Born the 4th of January, 1643, at Woolsthorpe, near Grantham. I am president of the Royal Society. But there's no need to get up on my behalf. I wrote the Mathematical Principles of Natural Philosophy. I said: Hypotheses non fingo – I do not invent hypotheses. In the fields of experimental optics, theoretical mechanics and higher mathematics my achievements are not without importance; but I had to leave unresolved certain problems concerning the nature of gravitational force. I also wrote theological works. Commentaries on the Prophet Daniel and on the Revelation of St John the Divine. I am Newton, Sir Isaac Newton. I am the president of the Royal Society.

(He rises and goes into his room.)

EINSTEIN. I am Einstein. Professor Albert Einstein. Born the 14th of March, 1879, at Ulm. In 1902 I started work testing inventions at the Federal Patent Office in Berne. It was there that I propounded my special theory of relativity which changed our whole concept of physics. Then I became a member of the Prussian Academy of Science. Later I became a refugee. Because I am a Jew. It was I who evolved the Formula $E = mc^2$, the key to the transformation of matter into energy. I love my fellow-men and I love my violin, but it was on my recommendation that they built the atomic bomb. I am Einstein. Professor Albert Einstein, born the 14th of March, 1879, at Ulm.

(*He rises and goes into his room. He is heard fiddling. Kreisler. Liebesleid.*)

MÖBIUS. I am Solomon. I am poor King Solomon. Once I was immeasurably rich, wise and God-fearing. The mighty trembled at my word. I was a Prince of Peace, a Prince of Justice. But my wisdom destroyed the fear of God, and when I no longer feared God my wisdom destroyed my wealth. Now the cities over which I ruled are dead, the Kingdom that was given unto my keeping is deserted: only a blue shimmering wilderness. And somewhere round a small, yellow, nameless star there circles, pointlessly, everlastingly, the radioactive earth. I am Solomon. I am Solomon. I am Solomon. I am poor King Solomon.

(*He goes into his room. Now the drawing-room is empty. Only Einstein's fiddle is heard.*)